D1398663

ABOUT THE COVER: *The Roman Forum in imperial times. In the little circular temple of Vesta, the sacred fire on the city's official hearth was kept burning continuously for 1100 years by the vestal virgins.*

ACKNOWLEDGMENTS: *Alinari/Art Reference Bureau: 14. American Archives of World Art: 12. Chase Manhattan Bank Money Museum: 34B. Kunsthistorisches Museum, Vienna; photo by Francis G. Mayer: 31 TL. Metropolitan Museum of Art, Rogers Fund, 1906: 31. Metropolitan Museum of Art, Rogers Fund, 1914: 33 TC. Musei Capitolini, Rome: 11 TR. Museo Nazionale, Naples: 11 TL. Museo Nazionale, Naples, European Art Color Slide Co.: 29. Toledo Museum of Art, gift of Edward Drummond Libbey; photo by Museum Color Slide Assoc., Boston: 33R. The Uffizi Gallery, Florence: 11C. Wadsworth Atheneum, Hartford, photo by Francis G. Mayer: 33BC.*

ANCIENT ROME

by ROGER BUTTERFIELD

illustrated by PETER SPIER

THE ODYSSEY PRESS · NEW YORK

> *"Rome is a citadel which has all the peoples of the Earth for its villagers."*—ARISTIDES OF SMYRNA, 2ND CENTURY A.D.

At the height of Rome's grandeur all the roads of the empire led to the Millareum Aureum (Golden Milestone), a marble column sheathed with gilt bronze which stood in the Forum Romanum, at the end of the Sacred Way. From this spot were measured the distances to the principal cities which were subject to Rome: Athens, Antioch, Ephesus, Rhodes; Alexandria and Carthage in Africa; Carthagena (Carthago Novo) in Spain; Marseilles and Lyons (Lugdunum) in Gaul; Milan, Aquilae, Rimini, Ravenna, Tarentum and Brindisium in Italy; Salona (near

The Forum Romanum, with the Colosseum in background, upper left; at upper right looms the emperor's palace.

present-day Split) in Illyria; Syracuse in Sicily. From here generals and governors set out to take their stations in the 41 Roman provinces and along the well-defined Roman frontier, which ran from Scotland to Arabia, from the Atlantic Ocean to the Red and Black Seas, from the German forests above the Danube to the Sahara Desert of Africa. For centuries under Roman rule, this heartland of Western civilization was better organized, more firmly governed, and certainly more united than ever before or since. ■ Roman dominion was based on conquest, accompanied by ruthless slaughter. Julius Caesar, who was no sadist, calmly set down in his *Commentaries* the results of his eight years' campaigning in Gaul: 800 towns

7

The hills of Rome were originally seven in number, but as the city grew it embraced ten heights, on both sides of the winding Tiber. BELOW: *Excavations have revealed portions of the first city wall (c. 753 B.C.) and burial urns which are believed to be copies of primitive Roman huts.*

and cities taken, 300 "peoples" subjugated, one million individuals killed, another million sold into slavery. No Roman statesman ever forgot the example of Romulus, legendary founder and first king of the city, who slew his own twin brother when his authority was threatened. ■ War and mass murder were common events in the ancient world, although perhaps no more frequent than they have been since. But the Romans did more than kill and be killed—they were passionate builders and organizers. They never stopped trying to make some sense, some logical and lasting relationship, out of the conflicts of men and nations. They clearly envisioned a unified world with an equal standard of justice for all. Their goal was stated by Cicero: "True law is right reason, consonant with nature. . . . This law does not differ for Rome and for Athens, for the present and for the future, but one eternal and

The symbol of highest authority in Rome was the fasces, a bundle of rods enclosing an ax. Consuls were entitled to 12 fasces, each borne by a lictor over his left shoulder. Praetors (city magistrates) had two, proconsuls in the provinces six. Only the emperor could display 12 fasces crowned with bay leaves. S P Q R—Senatus Populusque Romanum—was the Roman legions' insignia.

unchanging law shall be valid for all nations and all times."
■ The focus of Roman strength and weakness was the brawling city of Rome itself, whose peak population of perhaps 2 million (in 100 A.D.) was the greatest concentration of human energy since history began. Naturally, the Romans liked to believe that their city was founded on miracles. Yet its beginnings were probably the same as those of hundreds of other villages scattered through Iron Age Italy. A band of pugnacious shepherds marked off a space on top of a hill overlooking the Tiber River, built a mud wall around their huts, and made it their nightly refuge. They named the hill for Pales, goddess of flocks, and it became in time the Pala-

PLAN OF REPUBLICAN ROME C. 40 B.C.

1. Temple of Jupiter Capitolinus 2. Senate House 3. Temple of Vesta 4. Temple of Portunus 5. Temple of Aesculapius 6. Theatre of Pompey 7. Portico & Senate House 8. Flaminian Circus 9. Temple of Flora 10. Temple of Juno Lucina 11. Circus Maximus 12. Temple of Minerva 13. Emporium 14. Public Reservoir

The Senate, whose name was derived from senex (old man), was as old as Rome itself. For 600 years it held its meetings in the Curia Hostilia (BELOW), a plain white-washed building at the north end of the Forum. When this was destroyed in the civil wars Augustus built the larger Curia Julia to take its place. The military dictators "packed" the Senate, raising its membership to over 1000. Augustus cut it back to 600.

Under the Roman Republic the Senate had 300 members, many of whom had already been consuls, judges, or generals. Its meetings were called by a ruling consul who stood in front of the curving benches and listed the business of the day. Senators spoke in order of their seniority and voted by moving to left or right of the central aisle. In this chamber a group of senators surrounded Julius Caesar in 44 B.C. and treacherously stabbed him to death. The enraged Romans wrecked the building and added its wooden benches to Caesar's funeral pyre.

tine Hill, the home of millionaires, senators and eventually emperors only—the most exclusive real estate in the world. ■ The rise of Rome was not rapid. The Romans fought for 500 years to become the dominant power in Italy, and then fought for another 500 years to create and stabilize their empire. During this long time it was never true that Rome, in a military sense, was unbeatable. The city was captured and sacked by Gauls as early as 390 B.C. Hannibal destroyed three Roman armies and remained the master of Italy for years. Rome survived these and other defeats because of the self-discipline of its citizens and the resilience of its political system, which was the nearest thing in ancient times to modern representative government. The word republic (res publica—"public thing") was coined by the Romans to describe the way they ruled themselves during

Cicero

Cato

Sulla

Cicero was the Senate's greatest orator, Cato its sternest spokesman for Roman expansion; Sulla inflated its membership. BELOW: *The Tabularium, where laws were recorded.*

Bearded barbarians are lined up and beheaded after a Roman victory in 176 A.D. The victims were German tribesmen who violated the imperial border along the Danube River. The sculptured detail is from a column erected by Marcus Aurelius to honor his predecessor, Antoninus Pius.

the five centuries before the birth of Christ. ■ The primitive Romans expelled their last king in 510 B.C. In the republic, they retained their Senate, or council of elders, which consisted at first of the chiefs of the landowning family clans. The Senate grew steadily in prestige and authority; it was the voice of the Roman conscience, the sounding board of wisdom and patriotism, as well as the privileged stronghold of the rich patricians of latter-day Rome. But the Senate in fact never made any laws. That power was given by the people to two elected consuls, who governed jointly for just one year and according to law could not be reelected (although sometimes they were). The consuls were temporary kings who wore the purple toga and used the ivory chair, which had once distinguished the Roman kings. In addition to ruling the state, the consuls commanded Rome's armies in the field, made treaties of

Octavius Augustus, the first emperor, is depicted here as commander-in-chief of the legions, wearing a gleaming cuirass of gilded armor.

peace, enslaved conquered foes, and disposed of loot. As a rule they were elected from the membership of the Senate; at the end of their terms they continued to be lifetime senators and were often made military governors (proconsuls) of provinces as well. ■ The principal check to the consuls' power was a unique political office which the early Romans invented: the tribunes of the people. The tribunes' duty was to see that the *plebs*, or ordinary citizens, were not pushed around by the two upper classes: the patricians, who dominated the government and priesthood, and the self-made *equites*, or knights, who ran Roman business. A tribune could stop the arrest of anyone by placing himself in front of the threatened man. The tribune needed no armed assistants; his position was sanctified by religion. The penalty for attacking a tribune was to be put to death as a "sacrifice." ■ A tribune could not leave the city of Rome, and his house had to stand open day and night so appeals could be heard

Fresco from an Apulian tomb shows a funeral chorus of women in a ritual dance of mourning.

any time. At first, two tribunes were elected, then four, and finally ten. Their term was one year, and their authority did not extend beyond the city limits. But as the urban population grew, the tribunes became very powerful. They could prevent consuls from enacting laws which might harm the people by simply appearing and saying "Veto" ("I forbid"). Although they were plebeians themselves, the tribunes acquired the right to sit in the Senate and take part in its debates. They could summon the people to an assembly, address them, and call for a vote, even when the consuls disapproved. ■ The tribunate flourished 400 years, preserving a vital balance in the mechanics of Roman government. Its importance ended in 133 B.C. when a patrician mob cornered the tribune and reformer Tiberius Gracchus at the Cap-

LEFT: *Sacrificial table with oil and wine.* CENTER: *Altar in the Forum to "the unknown god."* RIGHT: *Household altar.*

itol and beat him to death with "fragments of stools and chairs." Despite the old religious laws the murderers were not punished. This, Plutarch wrote, "was the first sedition amongst the Romans, since the abrogation of kingly government, that ended in the effusion of blood. All former quarrels which were neither small nor about trivial matters, were always amicably composed, by mutual concessions on either side, the Senate yielding for fear of the commons, and the commons out of respect to the Senate." Henceforth the poor and the rich were foes, and civil war was almost continuous in the late Roman republic. The consular dictators—Marius, Sulla, Pompey, and Caesar—managed (rather than ruled) the city by playing one faction against the other. And so did the early emperors. ■ Yet even after Roman politics failed, the great city increased in majesty, and the empire reached its zenith.

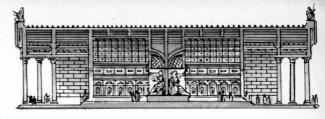

Rome's largest temple was dedicated to Venus, ancestress of all Romans, and to Roma Aeterna, genius of the city. Each had a separate cella, so the temple faced two ways. BELOW: *Sacred chickens whose choice of food was studied by augurs and might determine peace or war; crooked stick, or lituus, used to mark temple boundaries; and two flamines, tenders of temple flames.*

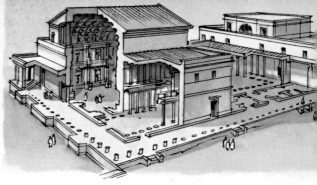

Roman reverence for law found majestic expression in the Basilica Julia, begun by Julius Caesar and completed by his nephew Augustus as a central home for justice. Here sat the Court of the Centumviri (actually 180 leading citizens) who divided into panels to judge important cases. When a lawyer was especially eloquent the judges rose to their feet and applauded. After such a triumph an attorney could count on quickly becoming a millionaire.

Cutaway reconstruction shows the Flavian palace on Palatine Hill, completed by Domitian about 90 A.D. At front is the enormous throne room, flanked by the emperor's household temple and a legal tribunal where he heard appeals. The building in the rear housed apartments and banquet rooms. Domitian had the marble walls polished so they acted as mirrors—to guard against attack from behind. But he was assassinated anyway, by a trusted servant.

16

The Palatine Hill now became one vast compound of palaces, temples, and government offices, an organized mass of marble and masonry, rising on tiers of arches and connected by forests of columns. Its rooftops gleamed with gold tiles and domes; its myriad windows were shaded by huge purple awnings. The whole area was reserved for the emperor and his bureaucracy. Hidden from ordinary Roman eyes were the interior gardens and parks and fountains, the rows of statues and choice works of art, as well as the sudden, messy scenes when one emperor was stabbed to death or poisoned, and another was raised in his place. ■ The imperial command post loomed above the city, aloof and omnipresent. A short distance away was a matching peak, the Capitoline Hill, which had once been the citadel of primitive Rome, and later the capitol of the republic. Between the two hills, squeezed in a narrow six-acre space, was the ancient *Forum Romanum*, where the Senate still had its meeting place but little of its former power and authority. In imperial times the Capitoline Hill and busy Forum were overloaded with temples and monuments which had some meaning in Roman

For centuries Rome had only wooden bridges across the Tiber, so they could be quickly destroyed during an invasion. ABOVE: *The stone Pons Fabricius, built in 62 B.C. and still used.* BELOW: *The dining pavilion of Hadrian's luxurious villa at Tivoli.*

100 B.C.

Temple of Fortuna Virilis

Circular Temple

Rome's public buildings, the largest achieved in antique times, were a true expression of Rome's wealth and power. They were made possible by a Roman invention, concrete, but were faced with brick and marble.

Arch of Titus A.D. 81.

Plan of Pantheon

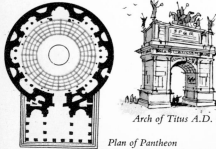

Trajan replaced by St. Peter

Light Openings

Stairs

Column of Trajan A.D. 114

folklore but which were mostly built for show. They cost a great deal of money, and the total architectural effect was awesome. A British chieftain, Caractacus, who saw all this splendor as a prisoner of war, was said to have asked his Roman guards: "How is it possible that you, who have such magnificent palaces, should envy us our poor huts?" ■ The answer might well have been that the later Romans didn't really covet any barbarian huts. But they were impelled by economic necessity to safeguard their empire and stamp out revolts. As early as the 2nd century B.C., Rome was no longer a self-sufficient community; when the grain ships failed to arrive from Egypt, the urban population went hungry. The wealth and commerce which regularly poured into Rome depended on roads and bridges and harbors, on prosperous provinces and thriving cities, on peaceful conditions throughout the empire. These things the imperial administration provided, even under the worst emperors. ■ It should also be said that a number of emperors—the ones who ruled longest and died natural deaths—were wise, able, conscientious men. Augustus, the first, put an end to the old Roman policy of plundering the provinces. He appointed career governors, paid them a fixed salary, and did not permit them to rob the inhabitants. Successful governors were retained for long terms; under the republic they served only one year, and would often instigate war or revolt just to obtain an easy triumph with all its accompanying loot. ■ Tiberius, who followed Augustus, was especially harsh with the Roman patricians, who were anxious to extort more taxes from the provinces. "A good shepherd," he warned, "shears his sheep: he does not skin them." He described better than anyone else ever has the nature of his job. "The em-

The basilica, with a plan probably derived from the Greek temple, was used by the Romans as a hall where justice was administered and business transacted. The Basilica of Constantine, which was built adjoining the Forum in 312 A.D., foreshadowed Gothic architecture in its structure; piers were employed to take thrust and weight of the vaults.

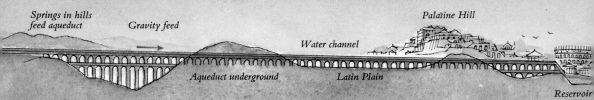

Springs in hills feed aqueduct

Gravity feed

Palatine Hill

Water channel

Aqueduct underground

Latin Plain

Reservoir

The eleven aqueducts which watered Rome were marvels of engineering grace and precision. They strode across valleys on tall arches of stone and tunneled through hills, still supported by arches, but always maintaining a gentle downhill flow. The Claudian aqueduct (52 B.C.) began some 42 miles from Rome, passed under the templed Capitoline Hill and ended near the old Roman Forum.

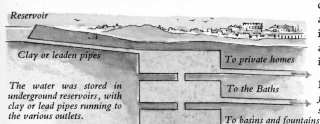

Reservoir

Clay or leaden pipes

To private homes

The water was stored in underground reservoirs, with clay or lead pipes running to the various outlets.

To the Baths

To basins and fountains

pire," he said, "is a wolf which I hold by the ears!" ■ The imperial reforms touched off a universal surge of prosperity which lasted almost 300 years. The provinces now kept most of their revenues and spent them for improvements at home. Gaul, Spain, Africa, Illyria developed into rich and prosperous countries, as important to the empire's well-being as Italy itself. Old Roman army camps grew into cities, and some of these have become modern capitals: Londinium (London), Lutetia (Paris),

RIGHT: *Even emperors stripped and dipped with their subjects in the vast luxury of the public baths. Cutaway view shows structure of Diocletian's baths.*

Vindobono (Vienna), Singidinum (Belgrade) and others. ■ The Roman genius expressed itself best in practical engineering projects. Sextus Frontinus, water commissioner of the city of Rome, was bursting with pride in 97 A.D. when he wrote a book about his great aqueducts. "Will anybody," he asked, "compare the idle Pyramids, or those other useless though renowned works of the Greeks with these aqueducts, these many indispensable structures?" Rome's water supply was indeed a marvel; in Frontinus' time it delivered an estimated 300 million gallons a day, or about 150 gallons for every man, woman and child in Rome. This is the same proportionate amount which is used for all purposes—domestic, commerical, and industrial—in present-day New York City. ■ Water was free to all in Rome. Most people got their supply at one of the 13,000 public fountains and carried it home. There were never more than 1,000 private homes which had water piped in; these were luxurious mansions and palaces with dozens of taps, suites of marble-lined bathrooms, and toilets flushed

"In what rented apartment is sleep possible?" groaned Juvenal in 100 A.D. At night Rome teemed with rowdy crowds and the clamor of wheeled traffic, which was not permitted on the streets by day.

Most Romans lived in blocks of walkup apartments (insulae) built of concrete reinforced with wood. Because so many dwellings collapsed or burned, Augustus limited their height to 70 feet. On the first floor a middle-class family with 10 slaves paid $35 a month for comfortable quarters. Rooms at the undesirable top rented for $5 or less.

The population of ancient Rome (RED AREA ABOVE) was about equal to that of the modern city (BROWN AREA). Some population figures during 1800 years:

100 A.D. (estimated) . 2,000,000
546 A.D. (for 40 days) . . None
1350 A.D. 10,000
1929 902,000
1964 2,000,000

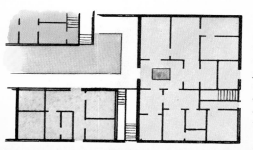

Floor plans of Roman apartments of the 2nd century A.D. resemble those of today. Some were duplexes; some had access to a private garden; some contained a private courtyard with fountain.

23

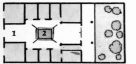

A Roman private home was designed to face inward on a cool courtyard or atrium (1) rather than toward the street. A central feature was the impluvium *(2) or reservoir for rain water. At left, a model and plan of the home of a well-to-do Roman of the age of Hannibal. Below, a much more elaborate* domus *of a wealthy merchant under Hadrian.*

with running water. Ordinary citizens who lived in apartment houses (*insulae*) paid a small copper coin to visit the public baths, which, under the emperors, became the most conspicuous buildings in Rome. The Baths of Caracalla (216 A.D.) occupied a site of some 28 acres (nearly five times as big as the whole Roman Forum) and served 1600 bathers at a time. The Baths of Diocletian, built 90 years later, were even bigger and could accommodate 3200 customers. ■ To the urban Romans a frequent bath was both a hygienic duty and a relaxing diversion. The baths were the community clubhouses of the Roman people—they served the same social purpose as the medieval cathedral, the Bavarian beer hall or the American movie palace of the 1920's. They were handsome, light-flooded buildings which teemed with comings and goings of citizens.

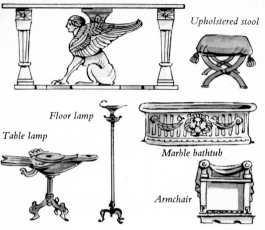

Greek table with sphinx

Upholstered stool

Floor lamp

Table lamp

Marble bathtub

Armchair

A great change in Roman living habits began about 200 B.C., when conquests in Greece, Asia and Africa introduced new luxuries. Furniture in the homes of the rich now followed Greek and Egyptian patterns.

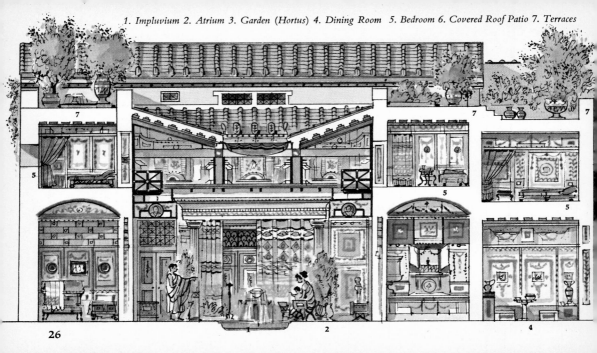

1. Impluvium 2. Atrium 3. Garden (Hortus) 4. Dining Room 5. Bedroom 6. Covered Roof Patio 7. Terraces

26

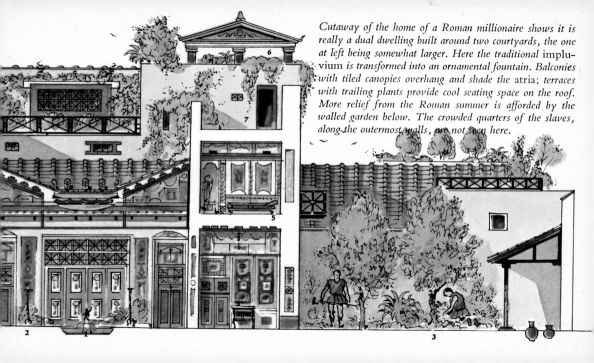

Cutaway of the home of a Roman millionaire shows it is really a dual dwelling built around two courtyards, the one at left being somewhat larger. Here the traditional impluvium is transformed into an ornamental fountain. Balconies with tiled canopies overhang and shade the atria; terraces with trailing plants provide cool seating space on the roof. More relief from the Roman summer is afforded by the walled garden below. The crowded quarters of the slaves, along the outermost walls, are not seen here.

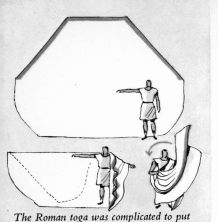

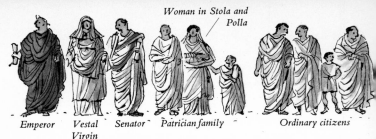

Woman in Stola and Polla

Emperor   Vestal Virgin   Senator   Patrician family   Ordinary citizens

Roman society was sternly divided into classes, indicated by dress. Only high officials and boys under 14 wore all-purple togas. Vestal virgins and senators were entitled to purple stripes. Ordinary citizens wore white. Even shoes (BELOW) denoted rank: red sandals for patricians, spiral straps for senators, plain boots for citizens.

The Roman toga was complicated to put on and uncomfortable to wear, but tradition insisted on it for all public and social occasions. Wrapped twice around the body and arranged in many symbolic ways, its folds might suggest, in the case of a senator, his attitude toward a pending law. The sleeveless tunic under the toga was Rome's national garment, worn at home by everybody, but in public only by slaves and foreigners.

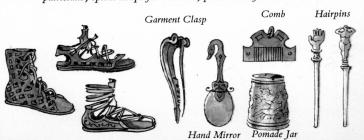

Garment Clasp   Comb   Hairpins

Hand Mirror   Pomade Jar

They had tennis and wrestling courts to work up a sweat, special rooms for annointing with oily soap or rubbing with sand (when you were especially dirty), steam rooms and hot air rooms, and chambers where water at various temperatures was poured over the body. This was done by an attendant; the Romans followed Hippocrates' advice that "the person who takes the bath should be orderly and reserved in his manner, should do nothing for himself, but others should pour water upon him and rub him." ■ The time for bathing was the afternoon, before the final meal of the day. The Roman work day began at dawn and ended at one or two o'clock. The baths, *thermae*, opened at noon. From then until dusk they hummed with conversation and gossip; a com-

Roman citizen and his wife, shown in a painting from Pompeii, may have been scribes or poets. She holds a tablet and stylus; he has a rolled-up scroll.

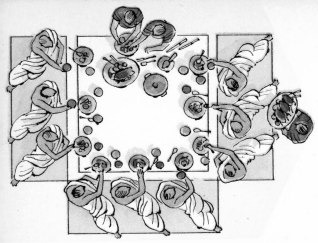

At formal Roman dinners nine persons reclined, three to a couch, around a low square table. Slaves brought the food to the open side. The host usually took the upper right seat; the guest of honor took the upper left so he could see everyone else without twisting his neck.

plete bath with rubbings and scrapings could take several hours. The Roman water system and sanitary habits were introduced everywhere in the empire. Roman aqueducts were built for at least 50 cities; they are still being used at a number of places, including Athens, Constantinople, and Segovia. In Britain, the homesick Romans built famous baths at Aquae Sulis (the present city of Bath), which are still filled through their original conduits. Roman officials in cold and foggy Britain equipped their homes with hot air furnaces and pipes for central heating—a convenience which vanished from the British scene when the Romans left in 401 A.D. and is rarely seen there even today. ■ It is well known that the Romans created little that was strikingly new in art, literature, philosophy, science, or the more subtle aspects of architecture. But in making life convenient and comfortable, in creating systems of communication and travel, in the durability and monumental scale of their public works, their achievements were never equalled until late modern times. In the high noon of the empire there were 50,000 miles of public highways, of which 13,000 were in present-day France and 5,000 in Britain. Letters and travelers moved from London to Rome more swiftly and easily in the 1st century A.D. than at the start of the 19th. The Romans invented the forerunner of the modern newspaper—the *Acta Diurna* (Daily Doings)—which was posted each day in the Forum and circulated through copies and letters. ■ The emperors encouraged local self-government wherever they believed it was safe. Gaul had its own provincial legislature; many large cities in all parts of the empire were

RIGHT: *Detail of handle of silver bowl, 1st century A.D., shows elaborate embossing of hunting scene.*

Armband

Ring

Earrings

Idle patricians in imperial Rome squandered fortunes on jewelry. One drank a huge pearl dissolved in vinegar, and boasted he had swallowed a million sesterces ($40,000).

Tablet and stylus

Scroll

Pen

Inkstand

Detail of papyrus

Busy Romans scribbled notes and memoranda on wax tablets with an iron stylus. Their books were long scrolls of papyrus, made by gluing thin strips of Egyptian fiber crosswise in several layers. These were attached to bone or wood handles and read by continuous unwinding. Mostly they were written in Greek, or copied from Greek texts.

Scrolls in container

Greek culture and science predominated in Rome. The clepsydra (water clock) below was a Greek invention.

Water clock

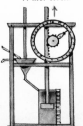

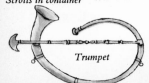
Trumpet

Lyre

independent in municipal affairs. Civil rights were extended until, in 212 A.D., all free persons who lived in the empire were granted the title of Roman citizens, with equal standing in the courts. ■ This privilege did not include slaves, who by this time were very numerous in Italy and did all the hard work on the farms and in city homes and offices. The Romans, of course, did not invent slavery. Like all men who ever owned slaves, they could argue that they inherited the system. And slavery as it existed in Rome was different from the black slavery that developed later in America. Rome's slaves were of all colors and nations; there was no prejudice against them on either account. There were many skilled and even gifted slaves: doctors, teachers, actors, musicians, barbers, and accountants. Epictetus, the Stoic philosopher, was one of thousands of learned Greeks who, because of the fortunes

Greek influence is evident in Roman bust of Agrippa, vase, and statuette.

Engraved Roman cameo of the 1st century A.D. is traditionally Greek in style and was probably made by Greek artists. The top half shows Tiberius leaving his chariot in the presence of his stepfather Augustus and other deities. Below, his soldiers prepare for a triumph surrounded by kneeling barbarians.

Rome was the world's greatest market place. ABOVE: *A warehouse on the Tiber, and conical mills to grind Egyptian wheat.* LEFT: *Shops of Trajan's forum, whose wares included silk from China and pearls from Ceylon.* BELOW: *A few of the many coins of silver and gold used in Rome.*

of war, lived for years as a slave in Rome. ■ Yet slavery was a monstrous evil in Rome, as much for what it did to the Romans as for what it did to the slaves. It was a blind spot in the Roman character that was never cleared away. Even Cicero was coldly contemptuous of the kind of labor the slaves performed. "We condemn," he wrote, "the base and menial work of unskilled laborers; for the very wages which the laborer receives are a badge of his slavery." And Cato the Censor, the very embodiment of Roman patriotism and civic righteousness, hastened to sell his slaves before they got sick and needed his support. "It is a good plan," he said, "to sell old cattle, old junk, and old slaves." ■ Much of the debauchery and senseless extravagance among upperclass Romans

A Roman triumph after a major victory parades along the Sacra Via to the temple of Jupiter, high at left. Captive kings were led in chains and later starved or strangled.

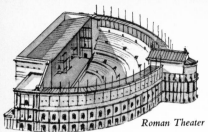

Roman Theater

Plays were never as popular among the Romans as brutal gladiatorial combats and races. Yet huge open air theatres, seating 20,000 people or more, were erected in Rome and other cities. The performances given there were free, paid for by public officials as part of the process of winning popularity and higher office. Roman taste ran to heavy farce with much coarse language and horseplay.

Theatre tickets, of metal or bone, were marked on one side to show section and row.

Cutaway view showing stage at left

Masks denoting comic or tragic roles, long worn by Greek actors, were mostly used for satire by the Romans.

in imperial times, the cruelty of the gladiatorial games, the public slaughter of men and rare animals to make a Roman holiday, resulted simply from the fact that so many people had so little to do. The emperor's officials ran the empire, and the slaves did almost everything else. The situation was not so bad in the provinces, where slavery existed but had not displaced individual farmers and businessmen.

■ Slavery weakened the empire and helped bring about its historic fall. But other factors were at least as important: corruption and gangsterism in the army, race suicide among the ruling class, a terrible epidemic of plague which wiped out half of Italy's population in the 2nd century A.D., the rise of militant

A mock sea battle drew 90,000 to the flooded Colosseum, protected by a canvas "roof" rigged by sailors of the fleet. In one such spectacle, 3000 men were killed or drowned.

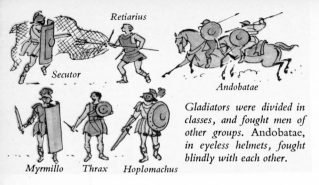

Retiarius

Secutor

Andobatae

Myrmillo   Thrax   Hoplomachus

Gladiators were divided in classes, and fought men of other groups. Andobatae, in eyeless helmets, fought blindly with each other.

Christianity which, for the first time in Roman history, led to religious civil wars. ■ The principal cause, however, was the never-ending population explosion among the so-called barbarians from above the Danube and beyond the Rhine. These Teutons, Cimbri, Heruli, Vandals, Goths, Marcomanni, Lombards, Burgundians and Franks—as various divisions of them were named—were tall, warlike, determined men with blue eyes and red or yellow hair. They ate raw beef, drank mead and beer, and migrated by the hundreds of thousands looking for new lands to farm. They crucified Roman merchants and cut out the tongues of Roman lawyers—"Now hiss, you vipers," they jeered. They brought their dogs and families with them in leather-covered wagons drawn by oxen. As long as they were let alone they did not usually fight the Romans. But they would not obey them either. They elected their own kings on the basis of physical strength and force of character, as once the primitive Romans had done. ■ For centuries these unwelcome visitors tormented Roman armies and emperors. They roamed through Gaul, Spain, Italy, the Balkans, and Greece, even into Asia Minor and Africa. The Romans exterminated whole nations of them, but they kept on com-

Blood cemented the Roman empire; blood was the favorite spectacle of the Roman masses. The earliest public games (ludi) celebrated religious holidays and were devoted to feats of skill. Under the empire they degenerated into senseless carnage. Gladiators not only killed each other but were pitted against lions, leopards and bears trained to feed on human flesh. Women prisoners were fastened to posts and torn apart by animals. Trajan gave one set of games that lasted 122 days and killed off 11,000 people.

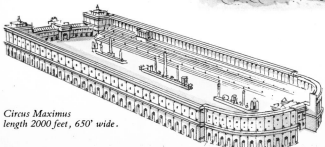

Circus Maximus
length 2000 feet, 650' wide.

Chariot races were the only events that outdrew the gladiatorial combats. Crowds of up to 385,000 went mad with excitement as the tough professional drivers whipped their four-horse teams around the tall metae (bumper posts) at either end of the Circus Maximus. No rule prevented a driver from blocking another, or hooking wheels and swerving to disable a rival.

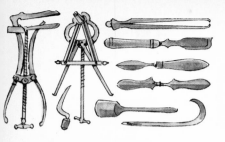

The Romans, said Pliny, survived without doctors for 600 years. Medicine was scorned as a career. Most physicians were Greeks or household slaves whose instruments (ABOVE) came from non-Roman countries. The only "hospital" was the temple to Aesculapius, on a Tiber island (BELOW).

ing. They copied Roman methods of warfare, they joined the Roman legions by the thousands, and eventually they became emperors themselves. In the melting pot of the later empire, the barbarians were Romanized and the Romans were barbarized until they were indistinguishable. ■ The illustrious emperor Constantine the Great was a perfect example. Balkan and illegitimate by birth, he was proclaimed emperor by his father's soldiers at York, England in 306 A.D., fought three civil wars with rival emperors in Italy, Greece, and Asia, defeated the Franks in northern Gaul, established Constantinople as the new imperial capital, and murdered his son, brother-in-law, nephew and wife in quarrels over who might succeed him. He was always fond of his mother, however, and because she was a devout Christian he was baptized on his deathbed—the first of the Christian emperors. ■ Long before his death the city of Rome had ceased to be vital to the empire. Its fall is officially dated at 476 A.D., when the last Western emperor was deposed by a German barbarian who declined the title. The Roman Senate, which had dwindled to a mere city council, then wrote to Constantinople pleading that no

Carpentum, a luxury carriage

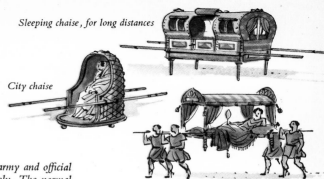

Sleeping chaise, for long distances

City chaise

Basterna, used by patrician ladies

Mule-borne litter

The great network of paved roads was designed for army and official use, although private travelers also used it extensively. The normal pace was 50 miles a day in Europe, North Africa and nearby Asia, but Julius Caesar once raced 700 miles, Rome to Geneva, in eight days in a stripped-down carriage, and one imperial messenger in Spain covered 336 miles in 36 hours. For city transport and short trips in the country, rich Romans depended on shoulder-borne litters and chaises. Because of narrow streets and dense pedestrian traffic, wheeled vehicles were not permitted in Rome or other large cities between sunrise and sunset. The emperor, vestal virgins, and generals and magistrates on special occasions were exempted from this rule.

"Once I was not; then I was; now I am not; but I don't care." So reads an inscription on a Roman tomb. Few latter-day Romans believed strongly in immortality. But all endeavored to plan for death; even the poor had funeral clubs which paid for pyres and burial urns. Christians, expecting to rise again, did not practice cremation. Their bones were laid on shelves in 600 miles of catacombs.

Columbarium (DOVE-COTE) was a Roman family tomb with enough niches for ashes of favorite slaves.

Hadrian's tomb, now Castel S. Angelo (RIGHT and CUTAWAY BELOW), had spiral stair to inner chamber.

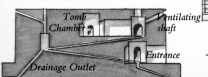

Tomb Chamber

Ventilating shaft

Entrance

Drainage Outlet

Via Appia

Cutaway at right shows four levels of the catacombs. There was space for 6 million bodies.

more auxiliary emperors be appointed for Rome. Having an emperor in the city had become a civic nuisance, an invitation to bloodshed and plunder. The request was granted. ■ Yet the empire itself lived on—for all of another 1000 years, the armies of the Eastern Roman Empire were a barrier of varying strength to the Asiatic penetration of Europe. And in Rome a new kind of empire was already in the making. The Christian Bishop of Rome—the successor of St. Peter—was now the leading citizen of the Eternal City. Even in disgrace and decay, there has always been a mystic power in the name of Rome. To the rising medieval kings of Europe, to the millions of converted barbarians, even to fierce pagan conquerors like Attila the Hun, the Bishop of Rome—who assumed the most sacred of all Roman titles, *Pontifex Maximus* (Chief Bridge-builder)—became the central symbol of Western civilization and unity.

All roads leading into Rome passed through cities of the dead, for cemeteries had to be outside the city limits. ABOVE: *The Via Appia.* BELOW: *Christian tombs with palms and doves stand near pagan tombs with dancing Bacchantes in old Roman cemetery underneath modern St. Peter's; steel beams reinforce foundation.*

CHRONOLOGY OF ANCIENT ROME

B. C.

753 (April 21): Legendary date of the founding of Rome. **510:** Romans expel their last king and set up an elective republic. **390:** Gauls capture Rome but Juno's geese give warning in time to save the Capitol. **338:** Rome destroys federation of Latin nations and begins the conquest of Italy. **266:** Conquest of Italy completed. **264:** Rome begins war against Carthage, in Sicily. **260:** First Roman naval victory, at Mylae; *rostra* (beaks) of captured ships are exhibited in the Forum and give their name to the famous rostrum. **241:** Carthage surrenders Sicily, which becomes the first Roman province. **228:** Carthage enlarges its empire in Spain. **218-215:** Rome begins second war against Carthage; Hannibal crosses the Pyrenees and Alps and destroys three Roman armies; makes his headquarters at Capua. **211:** Romans retake Capua; Hannibal moves to southern Italy. **204-201:** Scipio lands Roman army in Africa; Hannibal, "weeping with rage," returns to fight him and is defeated; Carthage sues for peace and pays tribute. **197:** Rome, using African elephants, defeats Philip of Macedonia. **189:** Rome destroys huge Syrian army and becomes dominant power in Asia Minor. **146:** Carthage is razed after third Punic war; Corinth, richest city in Greece, sacked by a Roman army. **143-133:** Portugal and Spain subdued. **133:** The tribune Tiberius Gracchus assassinated in Rome, beginning 100-year cycle of civil wars. **125:** Rome begins conquest of Gaul. **109-105:** Five Roman armies annihilated in Gaul by German barbarians. **107-101:** Marius, a peasant by birh, is elected consul; wins victories in Africa and Gaul; becomes dictator of Rome. **89:** Roman citizenship extended to all Italians. **88:** Greece and Asia rebel; 100,000 Italians slain. **87-82:** Sulla suppresses revolts and becomes dictator. **52:** Julius Caesar completes the conquest of Gaul. **49:** Caesar crosses the Rubicon to make war on his colleague Pompey. **45:** Caesar is made dictator for life. **44:** Caesar assassinated in the Senate. **31:** Octavius, nephew of Caesar, defeats Egyptian fleet off Actium; Antony and Cleopatra commit suicide. **27:** Octavius, becoming Augustus, begins imperial rule.

A. D.

9: Legions under Varus destroyed, ending Roman efforts to invade Germany. **14:** Augustus dies, succeeded by Tiberius. **43:** Romans begin conquest of Britain; Claudius is emperor. **64:** Nero blamed for huge fires in Rome; apostles Peter and Paul are executed. **79:** Vesuvius erupts, burying Pompeii. **114-117:** Trajan defeats Parthians, extends empire to the Euphrates. **122:** Hadrian builds a wall across Britain, marking northern limit of the empire. **212:** Caracalla extends Roman citizenship throughout the empire. **213-270:** Roman empire invaded from all sides by Parthians, Germans, Franks and Goths. **270:** Aurelian repels Germans in Italy and founds a line of Illyrian (Balkan) emperors. **313:** Constantine gives official toleration to Christians. **326:** Constantine founds Constantinople as new imperial capital. **360:** Julian the apostate becomes emperor; renews persecution of Christians. **382:** Gratian ends pagan worship in Rome; fire in the temple of Vesta extinguished. **401:** Romans evacuate Britain. **410:** Alaric the Visigoth captures and plunders Rome; spares the churches because he is Christian. **415-439:** Visigoths overrun Spain and North Africa. **452:** Attila the Hun invades Italy but turns aside from Rome on the plea of Pope Leo. **455:** Vandals under Gaiseric sack Rome. **476:** Last western emperor deposed in Rome. **486:** Clovis the Frank defeats Syagrius at Soissons, ending Roman rule in Gaul.

INDEX

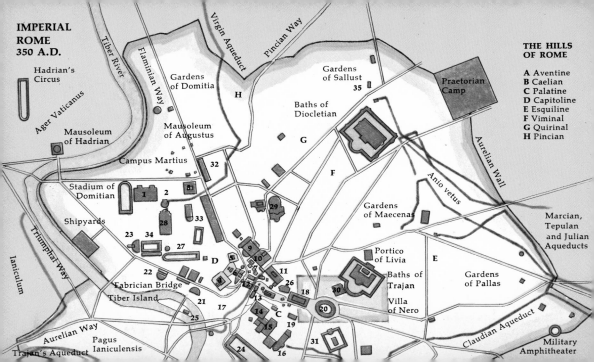

IMPERIAL ROME 350 A.D.

THE HILLS OF ROME

A Aventine
B Caelian
C Palatine
D Capitoline
E Esquiline
F Viminal
G Quirinal
H Pincian

Hadrian's Circus

Tiber River

Virgin Aqueduct

Pincian Way

Flaminian Way

Gardens of Domitia

Gardens of Sallust
35

Praetorian Camp

Ager Vaticanus

Mausoleum of Hadrian

Mausoleum of Augustus

Baths of Diocletian

Aurelian Wall

Campus Martius

H

G

32

F

Stadium of Domitian

1   2

31

Anio vetus

Marcian, Tepulan and Julian Aqueducts

Shipyards

28

33

29

Gardens of Maecenas

23   34

27

9

Portico of Livia

E

Gardens of Pallas

Iaculum

Triumphal Way

22

D

10

11

26

18

30

Baths of Trajan

Fabrician Bridge

12

Tiber Island

21

17

13

14   C   19

15   19

30

20

Villa of Nero

Aurelian Way

25

Pagus Ianiculensis

24

16

31

Claudian Aqueduct

Trajan's Aqueduct

Military Amphitheater